The Greatest Love Story In the Kingdoms of Heaven & Earth

MARCIA JONES

Copyright © 2019 Marcia Jones

All rights reserved. Printed in the United States of America. No part of this book may be used or reproduced in any manner whatsoever without written permission except in the case of brief quotations in critical articles or reviews.

For more information contact:
Marcia Jones
thegreatestlovestorybook@gmail.com
www.thegreatestlovestorybook.com

Published by: In Due Season Publishing LLC
Typesetting, Book Layout, Editing and Cover Design:
Enger Lanier Taylor for In Due Season Publishing
Huntsville, Alabama

indueseasonpublishing@gmail.com
www.indueseasonpublishing.com

ISBN-13: 978-1-970057-01-0
ISBN-10: 1-970057-01-7

Dedication

I dedicate this book to my children Amara, Jeremiah and baby Zoe (who is still in my tummy); and also to my Lord and Savior, Jesus Christ for rescuing me.

Once upon a time in the far away Kingdom of Earth lived a princess named Amara. Princess Amara lived in the kingdom with her parents; the King and Queen and her little brother, Prince Jeremiah.

One day, Princess Amara was walking in the palace garden trying to escape her little brother and daydreaming about who would be her Prince Charming. Her father, the King vowed to find her a suitable prince for her to marry, but Amara wanted her own adventure. She wanted to find her prince and write her own destiny.

Just as she was crossing the stream to sit under her favorite tree and daydream, as she often did in the garden, she heard a strange voice.

"Who's there?", shouted Princess Amara. "It is I, Prince Lucifer. I know your father is requiring you to marry the prince of his choice, but I think you deserve to find your own true love and have your own adventure." Prince Lucifer was very handsome and charming. Princess Amara didn't even think twice that he had appeared out of nowhere.

So Princess Amara stopped and thought about how her father had warned her of a mysterious prince offering princess's adventure and the freedom to choose who they wanted to marry. The prince was so handsome and charming that the princesses were persuaded to run off with him, but they would disappear, never to be heard from again.

But Princess Amara didn't listen to her father and Prince Lucifer said, "Just take my hand, and I will make your wildest dreams come true!" So, she did...

As soon as Princess Amara took Prince Lucifer's hand he changed into a fire breathing Dragon! She screamed and her little brother Prince Jeremiah ran out just in time to see the dragon take her away.

Meanwhile, in the Kingdom of Heaven, lived King Alpha A. Omega and Prince J.C. The King was also looking for a princess for his son to marry. He had found one he took to be a good fit in the Kingdom of Earth name Princess Amara. But to his disappointment she had been captured by an evil dragon and taken to the Dark Kingdom. Now King Alpha A. Omega was an all knowing King and he knew exactly how to get to the hidden Dark Kingdom so his son could rescue the princess.

King Alpha A. Omega began to explain to Prince J.C. that he would have to go fight and kill the dragon to rescue Princess Amara, but he might lose his life to save hers. But after Prince J.C. saw a portrait of her, he knew that he loved her and that he had to save her.

So, the next day King Alpha A. Omega sent off Prince J.C. with his Royal Advisor, who accompanied him to seek out the princess and rescue her.

While Prince J.C. and the King's Royal Advisor started their journey Princess Amara was praying that someone would come save her. She was being kept in the Dark Kingdom with all the other princesses that Prince Lucifer had tricked. It is there that they worked, day and night, in bondage.

Prince J.C. and the King's Royal Advisor had to travel seven days through mountains, valleys and forests to get to the Kingdom of Darkness, where the princesses were being held.

When they arrived to the Dark Kingdom they saw that it was a very cold and dark place where the sun never shined. It was always dark and nothing grew there. The land was deserted and sadness filled the air.

Prince J.C. wasted no time storming in to the Dark Kingdom to challenge the evil dragon, but what he found in the castle was a handsome prince. He drew his sword and told the evil prince that he was there to rescue Princess Amara and nothing was going to stop him. The evil prince let out a loud evil laugh and immediately changed into a giant fire breathing dragon.

Prince J.C. fought the evil dragon in an intense battle as all the princesses watched from afar. When Princess Amara saw Prince J.C., she loved him dearly and went to try and help him fight the dragon.

When the dragon saw her approaching, he went to breathe his fire in her path, but Prince J.C. jumped in front of her so she could run out of harm's way.

He ran straight towards the dragon so he could slay him. He pierced the dragon in the heart with his sword and with his final breath the dragon swung his large tail and struck Prince J.C.

Immediately, Princess Amara and the Royal Advisor came to his aide. But it was too late because the prince was not breathing. Just when it seemed that all hope was lost, the Royal Advisor bent down and blew over the prince. The Royal Advisor had heavenly kingdom powers and he breathed life back into Prince J.C. The prince rescued Princess Amara and all the other princesses from the Dark Kingdom.

Prince J.C. and the King's Royal Advisor escorted Princess Amara back to the Kingdom of Earth. Amara told her parents all that happened to her and how Prince J.C. defeated the dragon and gave his life for her and how the King's Royal Advisor brought Prince J.C. back to life!"

The King and Queen of the Kingdom of Earth were so happy to see their daughter again that they agreed to let Prince J.C. marry Princess Amara. The two were married and went away to the Kingdom of Heaven where they all lived Happily Ever After.

I hope you enjoyed this book. I want you to know that we all have a real life prince who saved us from bondage and from evil. In this story, Prince J.C. represents Jesus Christ. King Alpha A. Omega is Father God and the King's Royal Advisor, represents the Holy Spirit. The evil Prince Lucifer represents Satan and Princess Amara is a picture of all mankind and how Father God loved us so much that when evil Satan tricked us and caused us to be sentenced to a Dark Kingdom, Father God sent his Son from Heaven to come to Earth and die for every bad thing that we did or would ever do.

But don't be sad. He isn't still dead! In three days he rose from the grave! He paid the price for our wrong doings (also called sin) so we could go live in the Kingdom of Heaven and live Happily Ever After.

Princess Amara

Prince J.C.

King Alpha A. Omega

Prince Lucifer

King's Royal Advisor

God loves you very much and wants everyone to be a part of His family! Because of Jesus, all the wrong things you have ever done can be forgiven. God is just waiting for you to ask. When we tell God that we believe Jesus died for us and ask God to forgive our sins, He forgives us right away (Read 1 John 1:9 in the Bible). Once you are a part of God's family, you can talk to Him every day and be close to Him. You can look forward to living with God forever in the Kingdom of Heaven.

This is how you ask to become God's child:

Dear Heavenly Father, I admit that I have done wrong things and I ask you to forgive me of my wrongdoings and to help me turn away from them. I believe that your Son, Jesus Christ died for me and rose again. Thank you for loving me and giving me the gift of Jesus so I can live with you in the Kingdom of Heaven! I want Jesus to come into my life and be my Savior and friend. Help me to follow and obey Him, In Jesus' name, Amen.

Congratulations on making Jesus a part of your life.
Welcome to the Royal Family!

www.ingramcontent.com/pod-product-compliance
Lightning Source LLC
Chambersburg PA
CBHW060809090426
42736CB00003B/210